W9-BKG-428

Grocery Shopping with My Mother

Grocery Shopping WITH My Mother

POEMS

Kevin Powell

Soft Skull
New York

Copyright © 2022 by Kevin Powell
All rights reserved

First Soft Skull edition: 2022

Grateful acknowledgment for reprinting materials is made to the
following:
"A Poem of Friendship," copyright © 2013, leased with permission by
Nikki Giovanni.
"A Litany for Survival," copyright © 1978 by Audre Lorde, from *The
Collected Poems of Audre Lorde*. Used by permission of W. W. Norton
& Company, Inc.

Library of Congress Cataloging-in-Publication Data
Names: Powell, Kevin, 1966– author.
Title: Grocery shopping with my mother : poems / Kevin Powell.
Description: First Soft Skull edition. | New York : Soft Skull, 2022.
Identifiers: LCCN 2022023074 | ISBN 9781593767433 (hardcover) |
    ISBN 9781593767440 (ebook)
Subjects: LCGFT: Poetry.
Classification: LCC PS3566.O83253 G76 2022 | DDC 811/.54—dc23
LC record available at https://lccn.loc.gov/2022023074

Jacket design by Hilary VanWright
Jacket photographs by Evangeline Lawson
Book design by Wah-Ming Chang

Published by Soft Skull Press
New York, NY
www.softskull.com

Printed in the United States of America
10 9 8 7 6 5 4 3 2

For Vangie—
for reminding me what life-love was/is/shall be.

I don't want to be near you
for the thoughts we share
but the words we never have
to speak
—NIKKI GIOVANNI

So it is better to speak
remembering
we were never meant to survive.
—AUDRE LORDE

Some of these poems were previously published in/on the *Paterson Literary Review*, *Women's Studies Quarterly*, *African Voices*, MTV, PBS, *The Progressive*, *Ebony*, *Big Scream*, *Red Fez*, *Life and Legends*, *The Poet's List*, *A Gathering of the Tribes*, *Complex*, New-York Historical Society exhibit *Hope Wanted*, *Vibe*, *Fusicology*, onebillionrising.org, *When We Free the World* (book, documentary film, and podcast series), Deborah Bond's *compass: I* album, *Good Morning America* (ABC), *i am magic* (a choreopoem directed and conceived by Bridget L. Moore/B. MOORE DANCE), *Reflections* (a literary magazine of the United Nations SRC Society of Writers), the Freedom Cornerstone on the Downtown Greenway (in honor of Greensboro, North Carolina's civil rights history), *Arts-Today*, *2020: The Year That Changed America*, *The Brooklyn Rail*, 911memorial.org, goodmenproject.com, *HuffPost*, and *Poetry Potion*.

CONTENTS

Poet's Note   XV

SIDE 1

Grocery Shopping with My Mother   3

A Praise Song for Sidney Poitier   14

Happy   22

Brotha Man   25

For Miss Shirley LeFlore   30

For Miguel Algarín   37

For Cicely Tyson   40

Call Him D-Nice   44

For V (formerly Eve Ensler)   51

Dear Kobe   55

letter to bell hooks   60

Compass: I   68

For New York City   71

Hope Wanted   75

Our Mothers   77

The Beatles   79

SIDE 2

we them people	83
Tupac and Biggie	88
Haiku for Black Boys	98
Enough	99
Baseball	100
My Father	107
Janet Jackson Never Lies	111
When I Found Malcolm X	113
America	117
i am magic	123
Haiku for Vangie	130
Valentine Haiku	131
For You	132
Love	134
Jamaican Love Poem	136
A Love Sonnet	138

BONUS TRACKS

for aunt cathy	141
Reality Check	151
September 11th	155
Son2Mother	157
Acknowledgments	166
Self-Portrait	169
Kevin Powell's Previous Books	171

Poet's Note

32 of these 36 poems were written over the last few years, during some of the most difficult and introspective moments of my entire life. I am simply happy to be alive, truly alive again, and I am humbled to share them with you. Poetry is music and music is poetry, to me, and whether I listen to music when I am writing, or hearing dope or weird sounds in my head, no denying how necessary music is to my artist journey. That is why this volume is crafted like an album: there are 16 pieces for Side 1 and 16 pieces for Side 2; and the 4 selected poems— Bonus Tracks—were written between 1990 and 2008, when I was first an eager young poet, and then when I was a very intro- verted and very self-conscious older poet. I am equally grateful for the opportunity to share these selected poems with you as well. Finally, this is my 15th book and 3rd poetry collection, but the first gathering of any of my poems since 2008. I shall never abandon poetry for that long again.

kevin powell
New York City, the borough of Brooklyn
The year 2022

Side 1

Grocery Shopping with My Mother

1.

Dear God
please do not
take my mother
from me
any time soon
I am not ready
I do not know what
I would be without her
She has been my mother and my father
since she pushed and pulled me through her earth
the way a jagged little pill
shoves its way 'round the mouth of history
I love my mother like I love breathing air
even when she bruises me
with her words with her rage
My ma has forever bruised me
with her words with her rage

When I was a horribly lonely only child
I did not understand why
she behaved as she did
But when she got sick
really sick
a few years back
I was terrified
of losing my mother
I had her
speed-dialed to the hospital
there in Jersey
and sprinted me
as fast as I could to be with her
Ma said
it was the first time
she had been in a hospital
since she had given birth
And there she was
flailing like a caught fish on a frosty metal table
in an off-white hospital gown
her belly had
swoll so big
it looked like she
was pregnant with
me another time
And that is how it began
our regular trips
to the grocery store

because ma could not
move without immense pain
without waddling
like a penguin
in the middle of a summer hurricane

2.

Dear God
my mother does
not know that
I often walk behind her
on purpose
as she grabs
a pound of hamburger
a bag of sugar
a loaf of bread
a box of cereal
Aisle after aisle
my heart spills a bucket of suds
Aisle after aisle
my eyes spill two buckets of suds
like that day she
slid as a baseball runner would onto the floor
in her senior citizen apartment
from her favorite chair

and it took my entire back strength
to boost my mother's plump frame
to get her up to her recliner
And before I could
there we were one-two-three-four-five seconds
her on the floor me on the floor
when she and I
stared at each other
as we may have stared
at each other when I was
a scared baby and her a scared young woman
And in that very
moment I wanted to tell
my mother what she meant to me
but could not because
my mother and I have never hugged
have never kissed
have never said I love you
And here I was the caretaker
of a person who did not care to be touched by anyone

3.

Dear God
my mother's legs throb bad
Ma religiously rubs ointments on them

like she is scrubbing grime from her bathtub
She repeatedly refers to herself as being sick
She says she an old woman
She says she tired so so tired
She prays to you God from can't see to can't see
She says you will work a supernatural miracle
and heal her body Lawd
She says blood of Jesus each chance she thinks of it
like Jesus fixin' to be Superman
and jump off that prickly cross
My mother's altar
is the shopping cart at the supermarket
She baptizes the handle with one of her wipes
She cusses at me
when I ask her to pull her mask over her nose
She smooshes
her worn black purse into the child seat
where I once drooped my skinny limbs
She clutches tight the cart
says it helps her balance
Ma is afraid to fall
Ma ain't gonna fall in front of no strangers
My mother's power
is in the steering of the shopping cart
She pushes it forward the way
a truck driver inches their tractor
through bumper-to-bumper traffic
She wobbles slowly from the cart when she

spots an item she needs
three peaches
four red apples
five bananas
a package of chocolate chip cookies
a bunch of collard greens
a carton of orange juice
I straighten the crooked cart
that ma always leaves in the middle of an aisle
Hold my pocketbook
Watch my pocketbook
my mother chides me loudly
when she wobbles from the cart
Smashed inside her pocketbook
are those wipes and tissue and
cash and coins and her food stamp card
and clipped coupons lots of clipped coupons
and her crinkled grocery list
neatly written
in blue ink
Ma has the list mainly in her head
but sometimes glances at it
when her memory
is a throwback to the beautiful little dark-skinned girl
on that porch in South Carolina
But they did not tell little
dark-skinned girls they were beautiful back then
Ma thought only

White people and light-skinned Black people
were good-looking
They did not tell
little dark-skinned girls
they could be anything
So ma thought her life was
munching the raccoon meat
her desperate father shot and skinned
Life was daddy beating her
and her three sisters and brother
and her mother
as if they were slaves on an auction block
because life for every Black was one big beating
Ma thought life was signs and railroad
tracks that told her
where she could go
what her slipped joints could not do
was being branded
"tar baby" and "spade"
and "jiggaboo" and "spearchucker"
and ugly real ugly
by the local White folks
and the local Negroes too
just because she was born tobacco brown like James Brown
Ma ain't know nothin'
about no sexism or no classism
Ma ain't know nothin'
about bell hooks or Toni Morrison or Alice Walker

But she knew she was Celie before
Celie was Celie in *The Color Purple*
This
God
is why
to this day
I believe my mother loves Whoopi Goldberg
because when ma sees Whoopi in the movies
she sees herself crashing through
the broken glass of a dream deferred
This
God
is why Black people got therapy sessions
we name
field hollers
spirituals
the underground railroad
the blues
jazz
church
dance
the chitlin' circuit
prayer circles
funk
hip-hop
holy ghosts
barbershops
hair salons

Black Twitter
talkin' in tongues
laughter
the soul food
we squeezed between our chained ankles
and transmitted with us from Africa to them plantations
Ma be sayin'
we don't know nothin' 'bout no Africa
we ain't African
Ma don't know Africa all up in her
whenever she talks about the fish
she gonna lather and fry
about chocolate cake
she sacredly crowns with pecans
about potato salad
she will punctuate with sweet pickles
about wild and buttery cornbread
surrounded and lassoed from scratch
Food is my mother's best friend
because my ma
ain't got no friends
except her sister Cathy and me
Food is my ma's best friend
but the food has left her body wretched
like the planet
with diabetes
with high-blood pressure
with mysterious things she won't discuss

Dear mother
you are real mysterious
with all those doctor visits
like you're a bow-legged root woman
plotting potions
while lurking behind a sabal palm tree
Dear mother
you are real mysterious
with the inflamed whip marks of your past
held hostage in your bedroom drawer
Dear mother
you are real mysterious
while heavy living room curtains
smother your sunlight and your loneliness
But you are not alone
We are moon twins
emotionally eating our way
to the promised land
You told me food is your happiness
You begged me not to take away your happiness
I will not mother I will not
I see your beauty and your genius
in the way you boil the water
in the way you season the food
in the way you create kitchen magic
as you did when I was a boy
I smell the joy on your house dress
I feel the joy when you crunch and chew

I sense the divine when you suck on that chicken bone
And I know when the time comes
for God to look herself in the mirror
she will see you

Monday, January 10, 2022
10:14 p.m.

A Praise Song for Sidney Poitier

what kind of man
was he
money-poor Bahamas boy
airlifted from the womb
a few months too soon
during Evelyn's and Reginald's
mad dash to Miami
to hustle tomatoes
to survive
hardly weighed any pounds
teeny enough
to rest inside
the mud-soiled
palm of Reginald the father
what kind of man
was he
likely to be dead
in two or three days so his father
readied a shoe box
for the infant funeral
but the ears of
Evelyn the mother

clanged
of colonizers and overseers
in break-dance battles with
Maroons and Lucayan people
and her ears clanged too of a runaway ghost
slouching towards Bethlehem
while sheltering in Griffin Bat Cave
on Cat Island
The same Cat Island
her child will smell and
eat with his Caribbean eyes
the first ten years of his life
if she can resurrect him like Jesus
what kind of man
was he
Mother Evelyn's miracle
born yet again as she laid hands
on the congested pathways of Miami
her own private ghetto
knocking over the bowls
of Negro folks until a sister prophetess
struck a match with her mouth and foretold
the boy will live
and he will walk with kings
and it does not matter
that the boy's hair
is wooly like a seaman's cap
that the boy's feet

are bronze like tobacco-bleached grass
that the boy's face
is pitch-dark like a West Indian nightfall
that the boy's lips
are full like the stomach of a pirate's ship
that the boy's spoken-word poetry
unloads with thick African-English creole
because the boy
Sidney
is beautiful
like Black is beautiful
like the world before Columbus
and the trans-Atlantic slave trade
and its toxic residue
might have been
beautiful
because the boy
Sidney
was begat from coin-less dirt farmers
on an island with one thousand Black souls
and two White souls
and race was not yet a savage
interruption of his imagination
thus he registered all souls as all souls
he was merely
Sidney with flour sacks as clothing
who barely ever saw
reflections of himself

because the Poitier family of two parents
and seven children
had no mirror
had no nothing
what kind of man
was he
the first movies he witnessed
were wavy and jagged renderings
of himself in a pond
the first movies he witnessed
were wavy and jagged renderings
of himself in the shattered glass of a rum bottle
the first movies he witnessed
were wavy and jagged renderings
of Bahamian insects and birds and fish
breathing in the earth with their heartbeats
what kind of man
was he
The first sound that squared his
shoulders and yanked his head to attention
was the booming noise of nature's silence
The first sound that squared
his shoulders and yanked his head to attention
was the distressed plea
from his father
that 15-year-old Sidney go back to Miami
so that he the rebellious youngest child
would not dagger himself on that island

take care of yourself son
his father said to him
as Sidney was put on a boat
with three dollars and two years of formal schooling
the measure of a man
dripping with tears in the
mangled good-bye wave
of a parent who had done
what they could to prepare
a child for yesterday
what kind of man
was he
a teenage boy
with elastic troubles
in an outer space called Overtown
Miami's version of the barbed wire of racism
coloreds-only signs
as poisonous nooses hung tightly around the possibilities
of a people
they did not know you were
an under-educated man-child
who had never been told
what was impossible
they did not know you were
an under-educated man-child
unwilling to gash and stab
your own flesh with that barbed wire
that is why you fled Miami

for Harlem New York City
the land of Southern
and West Indian fugitives
the land of Marcus Garvey
and I-too-sing-America
blues and bebop revolutions
what kind of man
was he
if there was any life for you
your hands would have to make
that life happen
hands that washed dishes
became the hands banging
on the door of The American
Negro Theatre
became the trembling hands wrestling
with the words of a script
be an actor or be a dishwasher
a newspaper ad had
dry-cemented a seed that became
the rose that busted through concrete
those hands washed more dishes
but those hands were also held by an aging Jewish
co-worker who decided to help
you conquer reading
night after night after work
those hands touched and grabbed
syllables

those hands funneled and fed
sentences
those hands retrieved and embraced
new meanings
those hands raised the banner on a life-long
unity with Harry Belafonte
and those hands spun the knob
of a radio so that you could
learn how to speak
as a Shakespearean actor might speak
as Paul Robeson or Spencer Tracy might speak
as kings and presidents might speak
as Frederick Douglass might speak
after learning how to read as a slave
your freedom was in reading
your freedom was in speaking
your freedom was in acting
the urgency like sticks of lit dynamite
inside your membrane
I have to learn to read
to articulate me as a human being
what kind of man
was he
transporter of a nation
of millions on his watch
no eyes bugging out like a broken-back minstrel
no lips quivering like a terrified sambo
he the defiant one

with a patch of blue to garbage can his rage
the martin luther king jr. of American movies
Who I am is my father's son
I will scrub my knees with Porgy's shame
I will be a purple lily in the field of daisies
but I will also be a raisin
in the sun trolling like an endless road
I will sledgehammer my Paris blues
I will shape-shift my skin like sand
and slap a White man back
with such force it will echo through galaxies
from Chicago to Nigeria
to Brixton
a slap so dope and layered by trauma ropes
that when I die
they will say
this is evidence of things not seen
that I was not your Negro
nor your Uncle Tom
they call me Mister Tibbs
I Sir Sidney Poitier
what kind of man
was he
I am the me
I choose to be

Friday, January 7, 2022
12:38 p.m.

Happy

I
would
be
forever
happy
if
I
could
be
that
yellow-eyed
black
bird
finally
released
from
its
cage
and
able
to
soar

freely
into
the
purple sky
any
purple sky
like
I
own it
without
any
worry
or
fear
that
someone
anyone
would try
to
harm
me
just
because
of
how
I
fly
or

the
color
of
my
wings

Thursday, June 4, 2020
6:41 a.m.

Brotha Man

Black boy . . .
Black man . . .
Black male . . .
Black as those
crying ancestors
hanging like
strange fruit
in the potbellies
of those faceless ships

but we still standing—

because we be like
gumbo and grits
and candied yams
and curry chicken
tap-dancing on the drum
of an African prince
rocking to the beats
of Kool Herc & KRS & Kanye & Common & J. Cole
means we be hip-hop and we be magic, too . . .

means humility . . .
means swagger . . .
means love . . .
means life . . .
means being complex . . .
means being as endangered
as this old rickety Earth
means being as dangerous
as the imagination
of someone-anyone
who wants Black boys and Black men
to consider suicide
when the rainbow is handcuffs
yeah
means being misunderstood . . .
means being happy . . .
means being sad . . .
means being angry . . .
means being mad stressed . . .
means being vulnerable . . .
means being
sugar cane and high cotton
and emmett and trayvon
blowin'
like big mama's laundry
in the wind—

means son, father, grandson,
grandfather, uncle, nephew,
cousin, partner, boyfriend,
husband, teacher, coach,
role model, mentor, friend . . .
means inventor, scientist, doctor,
lawyer, preacher, president,
entertainer, athlete, hustler,
construction worker, union member,
garbage man, janitor, bus driver,
maintenance man . . .

means freedom is
that stinging cool
when the barber
sprays and wipes
the shine on your fresh haircut
means being incarcerated . . .
means being formerly incarcerated . . .
means death row . . .
means strivers' row . . .
means playing
prison bars
like they prince's guitar
like they dave chappelle going too far
like they reverend neck-bone smokin' his cigar . . .

because we still standing—

means I read, I study, I travel . . .
means I work . . .
means I work not to be
someone else's creation,
someone else's fantasy,
someone else's toy . . .
means I am not
your boy,
or your slave,
or your prisoner,
or your caged bird,
or your thing . . .

because we still standing—

means I will not
just shut up and
dribble,
means I will not
just shut up and jump, man . . .
means
I
am
a
man—

means
I
am
a
brotha,
man—

Wednesday, March 4, 2020
9:57 p.m.

For Miss Shirley LeFlore

(March 6, 1940–May 12, 2019)

I want to say
thank you
Miss Shirley LeFlore
for being a supernatural word
warrior who
allowed your poet laureate tongue
to be baked and bronzed by
the smoke-y laughter of
sister-girl hair salons
and the ham-hocked hallelujahs
of ancient Black churches with
Black Jesus in their ancestral bones
just means you
done seen some things
that you knew
as a little Black girl
resurrected there in the gumbo pot
of African soul they
baptized Saint Louis

that you were born
to witness
the weary blues
of a people
who made high ways
from no ways
just means
you is fearless
Miss Shirley
you is mad cool
Miss Shirley
you is forever
Miss Shirley
like the sugary taste
of a ripened watermelon
busted open
the way
your poetry
busted open
your womanhood and your Blackness
and your purple majesty
as the queen
you were ordained to be
the way
your momma and your grandmommas
were queens
the way

your daughters
are queens
the way
Black girl magic
is Miss Shirley LeFlore
swinging and bebopping
from World War 2
through the soul struts of Vietnam
and Civil Rights
to the boom baps of hip-hop
and orange monsters in the
White House with crooked eyes
yes, the way
Ella Fitzgerald
Gwendolyn Brooks
Billie Holiday
Nina Simone
The wash lady
The numbers runner
and the school teacher were magical
'cuz magicians dare, Miss Shirley
like you dared
you made a march to Washington
you made a commitment to poor people
and the arts and the telling of
"it"
like it is

because you dared to believe
that art was for the people
all people
your people
your beautiful lightredbeigebrownchocolatedarkblack
people
"I am the Black woman"
you said, Miss Shirley
and the people's church said a-women a-men ashe
go on with your bad self, Miss Shirley LeFlore
teach us how poetry is
Buddy Bolden cutting a rug
with the blues of Bessie Smith and Ma Rainey
while Miles Davis and John Coltrane
blow segregated nightmares into the wind
move us, Miss Shirley
from Saint Louis to New York and back again
embrace the young poets of my generation and the young
poets of today's generation like they are your equals
make me feel like you are one of my mommas
you Audre Lorde Sonia Sanchez Nikki Giovanni
Mari Evans Amina Baraka Camille Yarbrough Maryemma Graham
sister-girls who survived
sick and tired of being sick and tired
to become, like that God they call her,
sacred healing women
keepers of our culture

protectors of our sanity
believers in the spiritual voodoo
we call freedom songs
Miss Shirley LeFlore is not
good enough for you any longer
you are now dancing with the ancestors
cool jerking and twisting your woman-child
around the sweaty nostrils of the sun
and you are now Saint Shirley
Shirley, yes, same name of my birth momma
you are
Black
you are
Beautiful
you are
Powerful
you are
Unapologetically free
a caregiver and a caretaker to the very end
I cried Saint Shirley when I was told
you left us
on Mother's Day
but then I smiled
because Black women
like you
are the mothers
of this nation

are the mothers
of this universe
if there were no you
there would be no us
none of us
so take your bow
and your grand exit, Saint Shirley
I see you with your pressed and creased angel wings
hovering over
Saint Louis
hovering over
America
hovering over
our sobbing hearts
reminding us
to kiss laughter daily
reminding us
that when we channel
rivers of women
we must drink slowly
from their eyes
we must swallow the juice from their tears
so that we can be
free
free
free
as you

Saint Shirley
always were—

Tuesday, May 14, 2019
3:13 p.m.

For Miguel Algarín

(1941–2020)

muchas gracias
mi hermano
is not
good
enough
for
you
señor miguel algarín
so I say
yo te amo—
and
may god, her
the ancestors, them
the universe, it
shovel
the heavy sigh
from your nuyorican gold
and decree to us/to you
there
where

you are
now
that
puerto rico is
not only gentrified
land
but also
the
original melting pot people that gave us you
y tainos
y africans
y spaniards
y roberto clemente
y salsa
y young lords
y hip-hop—
that you are
congas and tongue-tied verses
arroz con pollo and shakespeare
the boogaloo and the lower east side
papi
you are/were/are
a boricua poet laureate
with a voice like that
of an old school lion-god
atop a freedom train
they call words and feelings
you are/were/are

spanish and english
ping-ponging
mikey piñero
and nancy mercado
and me me me
si, es la verdad: poor folks like me me me
slamming off the walls of the nuyorican poets café—
racism could not stop you
homophobia could not stop you
el sida could not stop you
being kicked off the board could not stop you
cultural colonizers could not stop you
because
mi amigo
your flesh may be of fire and wind and earth now
but your last breath
just like your first
will forever be
our rican and our soul—

Sunday, December 13, 2020
9:14 p.m.

For Cicely Tyson

Girls
Women
Black girls
Black women
especially
rarely told
they
are
smart
gifted
beautiful
special
dope
all in a single, relentless breath
But you are—

Africa and the West Indies
hatched you in Harlem
when Langston and Zora
penciled the blues
and Blackness
into your diamond-slanted eyes

as Ma Rainey and Marcus Garvey
swayed and screamed that
little Black girls
like you
are stars wherever they are
not just the help
not just the mattress
not just the punching bag
not just the mammy
not just the poll watchers or the pole dancers
but miracle chocolate goddesses
who
overcame and overcome
human-made diseases
like racism and sexual oppression
to straighten and afro pick a world
where you
pose poetic and pretty-like for magazines
run miles and miles to rescue jazz kings from themselves
and spiritually anchor movies that make Black folks
sounder and sounder in them fields
on them buses
in them African villages
in them classrooms
through the violent and paranoid walls of history—

you are our history
Cicely Tyson

in your 96 years
you gave us
to us
the way our mommas
gave
to us
buttered grits
or breadfruit and plantains
on a Saturday morning
you gave us
to us
the way Harriet Tubman
gave freedom back
to a stolen people
who did not know
they were
suppose
to
be
free
you were/are our freedom
you were/are what freedom
looks like
when
a little girl from Harlem from anywhere
shaves her head bald
glues on eyelashes that tickle the sky's belly
squeezes her neck with jewelry from the motherland

stares quietly into a camera like the fearless queen she is
fact-checks anyone who thinks dark skin ain't the Lawd's
blessing
and sings the ancient and sacred words
of a woman who done seen some things
and is ready for her rest:
"I like me
just as I am . . ."

Friday, January 29, 2021
6:18 a.m.

Call Him D-Nice

(for Derrick Jones AKA DJ D-Nice)

Just like
poverty
and the sad killing
of Dr. King
could not stop
the explosion of
hip-hop
up in The Bronx
a global sickness
cannot stop
a deejay
pencil-drawn down
these mean streets
of New York
from
slaying
two turntables
vinyl records
a microphone

and that humble
motto
of hip-hop:
making something from nothing
while spoon-feeding it
to
a multi-cultural multi-generational
worldwide dance party—
call him D-Nice
or call him
a pure rebel
a radical thinker on
a musical level
call him
photographic savior
Basquiat's graffiti dealer
Yankee-fitted b-boy griot
who backflips multiple hats
while crate digging
our troubled water from the
sewer of this here club quarantine
ain't no fun
social distancing
ain't no fun
mad disconnecting
ain't no fun
hella blaming

D-Nice be like
Harriet Tubman
liberating beats along
the Underground Railroad
D-Nice be like
Puerto Rico Jamaica Carolina
drumbeat
calls
bouncing off
the walls
of slave quarter malls
D-Nice be like
New Orleans ex-slaves
scooping up
neglected instruments
and gifting
the universe
a jazz
we thought
we had lost in Mother Africa
D-Nice be like
Nina Simone/Sarah Vaughan/Billie Holiday
—NinaVaughanHoliday—
yeah
wringing the rag of a note
so much
you can swipe
the tears

slipping from the lyrics
God bless the child
who drinks black coffee
while wishing i knew how it would feel to be free
yeah
D-Nice be like
Motown and Berry Gordy
splitting the electric
hairs of history
with a sound
for this America that America
this world that world
until we realize
like love is love is love is love is love is love
music is music is music is music is music is music
yeah
D-Nice be like Kenny Rodgers
the gambler
who is homeschooling
that people is just people
we them people
and if you
a bandleader
like
DJ D-Nice
like DJ Beverly Bond
like Duke Ellington
like Ella Fitzgerald

like Nile Rodgers
like Chaka Khan
like Stevie Wonder
like Aretha Franklin
like Prince
like Erykah Badu
then you also is
and you also are
oxygen
yeah
relief
yeah
one nation
yeah
a doctor of love
who steers us
into Instagram
all the way live
and we sweat and shake like we sipping on the holy ghost
in kitchens
and living rooms
in bedrooms
and backyards
in Hollywood
and ghettoes
we be poor and we be rich
we be famous famous and we be 'hood famous
we be Michelle Obama

we be presidential candidates
we be workers on the frontlines
donating our lives
to catch and carry
virus knives
we be voters
we be voters
we be voters
with one hand in the air
waving it like we just don't care
9 hours strong
9th wonder and Questlove, what took us so long?
to dream America
to dream a world
where everything
gon be alright
yup, we gon make it, Jadakiss
because last night
i said last night
yeah
yesterday, yeah
today, yeah
tomorrow, yeah
a deejay
came in the form
of criss-crossing fingers and super-sonic soul
and
that

deejay
saved
our
lives—

Sunday, March 22, 2020
11:49 a.m.

For V (formerly Eve Ensler)

One billion apologies are due
to the women and girls
of the world
who are you,
and had to bear
sledgehammer hate
from the violent paws of men
even men we call
our fathers
I am sorry
your introduction to human-hood
was a biological not
bothering
and incapable
of taming his own traumas
but instead
terrorized you
with exploding hand grenades
chained to his teeth
you

a little girl
whose body
was lit a-fire
whose smile
eyes
childhood
were hung and burned away
the way my ancestors
were hung and burned away
by nameless naked cowards—
I am also sorry your
mother
could not protect
you
because she too
lived in a land
littered with
rape and abuse
and revenge
a land held
hostage
by broken little boys
in men's bodies:
why does a monster
call himself a man?
why does a little girl
pray

that mister alligator
will rescue her
from a monster
who calls himself
father?
we wear
the permanently
bandaged scars
of our childhoods
as my mother wears
the rage and sadness
of what she might have
been
had girls like her
been encouraged
to be
not do
what freed you
what will free
women like my ma
was/will be the vagina monologue
scat-singing in tongues
like sister so-and-so
sifting through nature's church pews
for sanctified sounds
in the holiest city of joy
'bukin' cancer

'bukin' cancer
'bukin' cancer
from the body of the world—

Wednesday, October 20, 2021
9:15 a.m.

Dear Kobe

Dear Kobe,

Their eyes were watching
for you the way
they watch for Jesus Shuttlesworth
and Malcolm X and Nipsey Hussle
over on Slauson and Crenshaw
They came in cars
on planes by bus by grit
They got there by foot
They were in wheelchairs
Their sandpaper palms gripped canes and walkers
They were slouching Baby Boomers
salt-and-pepper-haired Gen Xers
tattoo-faced Millennials
They be Beyoncé
and Jimmy Kimmel
and 7-feet ballers who crush the ground
like jolly green giants
They marched from all over
with purple and yellow gold
steamed to their chests

they marched through
the musty scents of Downtown Los Angeles
the way 20th-century Europeans
marched from freedom ships to Ellis Island
the way 21st-century immigrants march
from Mexico into the barbed-wire borders
of the promised land
the way chocolate-legged country dwellers
marched from Mississippi
to the salty beaches and sleepy 'hoods of California
a massive army of humanity hemmed up
block after block
looking for the Staples Center
looking for that angel in America
who got a city of billions
'round the world saying
your name, Kobe
The lines of flesh speed text
as police and arena workers
shoo people to move like
you moved on that basketball court
a Black Mamba
yes
but also an African ballet dancer
who broke a-loose the chains
of plantations and copied and pasted Beethoven and basketball
with Biggie and Beverly Hills
as your body leaped and lunged

into the open mouths of nameless ancestors
who done seen some things
and them ancestors blew Michael Jordan
and Dr. J
and your daddy and your momma
and Philadelphia and Japan and Italy
and the holy ghost of Dizzy
and Coltrane into your veins
just means
the people marching to be like you, Kobe
and they be
White Black Latinx Asian Native American Pacific Islander
Christian Jewish Muslim Atheist Agnostic
This gender That gender No gender
They be Kendrick's cool hip-hop they be Sinatra's cool jazz
They be lakers matching jellybeans
with Amy Winehouse and Marilyn Monroe
as you Kobe and you Gianna wax poetic
with John Lennon and Marvin Gaye about love love love
They be a rainbow coalition
of thousands
marching over
your mid-range jumpers and 360-degree dunks
as they scrape field hollers and spirituals and your blues
from their veins, Kobe
Wearing number 8
Wearing number 24
Wearing Gianna's number 2

Street hustlers selling tee shirts posters
clipped and chipped memories of you
putting an entire nation on your shoulders
winning 5 championships
teaching us the magic of the mamba mentality
telling us to keep shooting
even when the odds are slanted
like that cloudy hillside in heaven
you be heaven to us, Kobe
'cuz you never gave up
That's why they come to you
like you are a saint a king
royalty
yeah
a political leader
yeah
a self-help guru
yeah
a storyteller
yeah
They come to you
because
you could
chest-pass a basketball
through the smashed windows
of centuries of dreams denied
They come to you because
you crumbled in front of us

and got back up
and confessed
and apologized
and sculpted yourself
into a husband
a lover
a father
a girls' dad
Vanessa Bryant's multi-lingual soulmate
her tears her words
the biblical permission
we need to release
your joyful angel's wings
into the healing arms of the Pacific
Kobe
forever
forever
forever

Monday, February 24, 2020
9:53 p.m.
Los Angeles, California

letter to bell hooks

my dearest bell:

I was not only a man-child
teething fractured knuckles
when I met you—I was also
an angry and misplaced
momma's boy, and you crushed
the cold ice beneath my holey sneakers
so decidedly that first encounter
as words such as
sexism and misogyny and homophobia
hemmed me up at da Lawd's crossroads
I am ashamed I cannot recall
that first person's name
who airdropped a sojourner's truth
into my concrete knapsack
because she was among the many women
of Spelman College I knew
back in the day
like Miss Kupenda Auset
who goaded me to become

something more than a man
Ayy, ayy, yeah, I was gifted photocopies
of your feminist candied yams
the way my ma shoplifted
reparation pennies so we could eat
My ma and her four sisters
and my Grandma Lottie
hot-combed and curled story after story
about the ways of White folks
about the ways of men folks
while I sat there and took it
yet I remained bone-thin
with bonier brain
when it came to understanding
that women folks ain't
just 'spose to be your momma
or your mattress or your
mule to punch and kick—

In the beginning
I was utterly frightened of your fearlessness:
Your Kentucky fried soul was un-digging
future and past generations
of women
long left for dead
Your Kentucky fried soul was un-dressing

future and past generations
of men
long left for dead
I was hunchbacked before you, and stark-naked
one of your books in my shaky hands
my unsalted ego crashing to the rug-less floor
like a beer pitcher full of lies
bell, I had already been
the devil's willing volcano
when I pushed a girlfriend
into a bathroom door
in July of 1991
that is why my body and mind
became a ferocious hurricane
when I first read you:
the ski mask was knifed from my face
the grime was sucked from my heart
the quicksand was scraped from my ankles
the clay was carved from my colon
a musty and sticky holy ghost triggered me
as my blood overflowed and retched
the absent father the single mother
the men on them liquor corners
the men in them barbershops
the men in them big positions
the communities the churches the chicken shacks
the reverends so-and-so the politicians no-and-no
the television shows the movies the sports the warts

the miseducation the ghetto plantation the prison cell
the swaying noose awaiting arrival of my neck—

bell, I remember we
sat down
greased elbow to greased elbow
a few years later
when I was writing for that magazine
I had never interviewed anyone
as brazenly free as you
one-woman emancipation proclamation
bold and snappy tongue
who painstakingly stiff-armed
capitalism and racism and toxic manhood
and politics and pop culture
like you were
the wind hurriedly washing away
the bulging whip marks of runaway slaves
I collapsed
in love with your genius
I dropped
my bags at your exposed feet
I stared
at myself with your x-ray eyeglasses
I shook and recoiled
whenever you scratched and peeled my history—

Oh, bell, you are gone,
and it is hella hard to write this
I jab these words with my half-crooked fingers:
I would not be the man I am without you
And you once said I was like a son to you
I am your son, bell, I am—

That is why
I am so terribly sorry I let you down
when I had to abandon
my trip to Berea, Kentucky
a couple of years ago because I had not
taken seriously what you
had sketched so many times about love
I was in a wretched place, bell,
my self-esteem
the bursting, rat-attacked garbage
in front of a Brooklyn bodega
But I still phoned you
every few months
simply to hear your voice
on your old-school answering machine
I was hurt and confused
as to why you never returned my calls
We had never gone that long
without talking in some form—

bell, I did not know you were dying—

Death embracing you like
a head-less family member
at an Appalachian train station
inside the home state you had fled in your youth
Only to return as an elder shero of the world
thirty-plus books in thirty-plus years
To die to sleep perhaps to dream
of a slow and methodical suicide
To die to sleep perhaps to dream
of a slow and methodical good-bye
to box and store
the great love-ship you never had
love hastily shedding pounds:
flesh draping your bones like a flimsy dress
love desperately crawling up stairs:
hands and knees like suction cups gripping a wall
I did not know bell I did not know—

I flew to Kentucky
through a diabolical tornado
I had no clue was happening
I was driven by Dr. DaMaris Hill
from Lexington to Berea to your house
on a block over yonder
I shall forget in a heap of tomorrows

I wandered anxiously around your 'hood
while you were prepared for the day's visitors
I was terrified of going inside
I was terrified of what I would see
I was terrified of what I would feel
At last, I was welcomed into your home
by one of your sisters and your literary executor
Original Black art over here
Buddhist symbols over here
Countless books like air tiles
to plug your home's lonesome spaces
You in a hospital bed in your living room
Tubes plunging from your nose
Cranky oxygen tank on the side next to your bed
Your hair totally gray, your body totally frail
I gasped and cried and cried and gasped
I was the only guest at that moment
bell, I got to sit with you for over an hour
I held and rubbed and squeezed your left hand
I held and rubbed and squeezed your left knee
I held and rubbed and squeezed your left toes
I gasped and cried and cried and gasped
I kept saying it was me
I finally made it to Berea, bell
You snored, you snored some more
When you did awake
you strained to unleash your eyes
I wondered if you knew it was me

You kept shouting "Let's go!"
as if you were ready to go somewhere
You kept saying "Yup"
whenever I asked you if you could hear me
That famously shrill voice as sassy as ever
I gasped and cried and cried and gasped
bell, I told you I loved you, several times
Then I did not know what else to say
As I arose to leave, I said a prayer
to the Goddess of wings and warriors
to safeguard your travel to the other side
I thanked you and I said good-bye quietly
I gasped and cried and cried and gasped
I knew I would never see you as flesh upon flesh again
And when I stepped out into the biting Kentucky air
I felt you strolling with me
bell, I hugged your spirit
Your spirit hugged me back
I gasped and cried and cried and gasped
And less than a week later, bell,
you had your freedom, at last—

Wednesday, December 15, 2021
9:25 p.m.

Compass: I

(poetic liner notes)

Say her name: Deborah Bond
(Da-boor-ah Bond)
Funkstress with the earth-angel vocals
of a soulfully jazzy fortune-teller naturally
Wandering through that universe they call
The DMV, but also a daughter of dust
they midwifed in New England
With tight and twisting hair stretching its roots
Straight into Africa. The woman: extroverted introvert
Who hums the same mystical air as Betty Davis
Chaka Khan Sade Anita Baker
Erykah Badu Jill Scott Sarah Vaughan Nina Simone
Her momma her grandmomma and them. Ain't no
Category and ain't no competition
for #BlackGirlMagic that trusts its internal
Compass to keep the time.
Time is her best friend.
Not where she been?

But here she is,
stride like a fly fashionista migrating from burden
To patience as if Harriet Tubman's running mate on the
Underground Railroad. Black lives do matter even
When no one is looking at the radio.
Yeah, the radio is her living room
During COVID because
the ancestors put a lightning bug in her
Ear that life is making something from nothing like
How we fisted field hollers, spit out spirituals,
Juked up jazz, baby-sat the blues,
rolled rock like a peace pipe,
And fortified funk with fish, grits, and hot sauce.
That is called love, smolder it in your chest until
Deborah's musical door stay ready for that manifestor to
Mentally spray collard green passion into her eyes
Eyes that are as much a
Self-aware Black mecca as atlanta
And this here music Deborah is gifting us on
Compass is like the cool breeze
Poetry of her yellow bell bottoms and never-say-how-high
Black-heeled shoes in that IG photo
Yeah, she and her art are free
Free as Janie felt after that Megabus journey
Zora Neale Hurston put Janie on
Yeah, Deborah's journey ain't been a crystal stair

But here this sweetly harmonizing butterfly lands
The musical director of her own freedom band—

Sunday, November 1, 2020
4:46 p.m.

For New York City

The Bronx—
richard avedon
snapshots of
prehistoric baseball games
and jewish b-girls and b-boys
of summer
jamaican hills that boogaloo-ed hip-hop
and doo-wop dreams
double-bagged
with spanish rice and beans

2.

Manhattan—
wall street

central park after dark
african burial ground
and faint native american sound
harlem a cousin of chinatown
as grand central plays the middle
solving this city's riddle

3.

Queens—
fingerprints on
south asian
spices and scents
baking inside
irish and greek
stews
as suburban 'hood
shimmies to the graffiti wordplay
of tony bennett
cyndi lauper
and nicki minaj

4.

Brooklyn—
a bridge begotten
by tongues
of the world
pride wide like
children's eyes
at coney island
spike lee and rosie perez
craving italian icies
on a roasted brownstone stoop

5.

Staten Island—
no human is
an island
neither is this landmass
wu-tang clan
holy-ghosted it
a kung fu flik
with ferry boat

and bleached picket fences
like its neighbor
jersey

Tuesday, June 16, 2020
7:30 p.m.

Hope Wanted

Hope Wanted
for New York
city
under
quarantine
like
gorgeous mosaic quilts
under
the
thumbs
of
somebody's grandmother
stitching pieces
of cloth
together
the way
her life
has needled and patched
star-spangled photos of
people
who done seen some things
who done survived some things

whose lives
are re-born
again and again
the way
a butterfly
can be hatched
again and again
from the cracked-egg concrete
of TheBronxManhattanQueensBrooklynStatenIsland
and rise
and rise
and rise—

Tuesday, June 30, 2020
11:48 a.m.

Our Mothers

(for my aunt, Birdie Lou Powell)

What would we be without you?
Even God herself
Knows that our mothers
Are miracle angels
Swiping away the sun's burns and tears
With their leatherlike hands
We mean
Mother mom ma mommy mama mami
Give birth to the earth daily
Transport the moon and stars on their backs
Work like hungry ancestors in orange fields
Smuggle their invisible dreams in swollen ankles
Sing blue songs that hang trees, double-dutch the breeze
And capture the motherland in a sneeze
We mean
Our mothers
Build and create and create and build
Things
Like civilizations and imaginations and love
Even when they get no love themselves

We mean
Our mothers
Are spirit and energy brushing buckets of paint
Beneath our feet
Means our mothers
Are magicians
Here even when they are not
Here even when they are not
Here even when they are not

Thursday, May 6, 2021
10:30 a.m.

The Beatles

I have been the walrus
I me mine
stumbling through
an octopus' garden
penny lanes and
strawberry fields forever
pen and pad in hand
liquid pain in quicksand
helter skelter my shelter
life a long and winding road
of yer blues
of all the lonely people
sadness a nowhere man
in a yellow submarine
on a magical mystery tour
across the universe
your music saved my life
yesterday
when you gave me a ticket
to ride poetry with lucy
in the sky with diamonds
your music

a revolution for a rubber soul
crying on those days
when mother shirley
told me let my father be
he is gone
I am the man
I wanted my father to free
Here comes the sun
Here comes the blackbird
sailing with
JohnPaulGeorgeRingo
into
something
I call
joy

Sunday, June 28, 2021
4:54 p.m.

Side 2

we them people

dream on
dreamer
the way Alvin Ailey
and Maya Angelou
and George Floyd
and Breonna Taylor
dreamed of
southern-baked
pilgrims
dancing and
slow marching
their sorrows
down the yellow
brick roads
of
second-line members
humming from
the heels of their dirt-kissed feet:
i wanna be ready/to put on my long white robe . . .
we are survivors
we are survivors

we are survivors
of people
who were free
and became slaves
of people
who were slaves
and became free
we know why the caged bird sings
we know what a redemption song brings
we them people
we the people
we are those people
who shall never forget
our ancestors all up in us as we sleep
our grandmother all up in us as we weep
because we are
native american
black irish welsh french german polish italian
jewish puerto rican mexican greek russian
dominican chinese japanese vietnamese
filipino korean arab middle eastern
we are biracial and we are multicultural
we are bicentennial and we are new millennial
we are essential and we are frontline
we are everyday people and we are people everyday
we are #metoo we are #metoo we are #metoo
we are muslim christian hebrew too

we are bible torah koran atheist agnostic truer than true
we are rabbis and imams and preachers and yoruba priests
tap-dancing with buddhists and hindus and rastafarians
as the Nicholas Brothers
jump and jive and split the earth in half
while Chloe and Maud Arnold
them syncopated ladies
twist and shout and stomp and trump
hate
again—
again—
again—
yeah
still we rise still we surprise
like we got Judith Jamison's crying solo in our eyes
every hello ain't alone every good-bye ain't gone
we are every tongue every nose every skin every color every face mask
we are mattered lives paint it black
we are mattered lives paint it black
we are mattered lives paint it black
we are every tattoo every piercing every drop of blood
every global flood
we are straight queer trans non-gender conforming
we are she/he/they
we are disabled abled poor rich
big people little people in between people
we are protesters pepper-sprayed with knees on our necks

we are protesters pepper-sprayed with knees on our necks
we are protesters pepper-sprayed with knees on our necks
we them people
we the people
we are those people
who will survive
these times
because we done
survived
those times
where pandemics were
trail of tears and lynchings and holocausts
where pandemics were
no hope and no vote and no freedom spoke
we them people
we the people
we are those people
while our planet gently weeps
we bob and bop
like hip-hop
across the tender bones
of those tear-stained photographs
to hand to
this generation
the next generation
those revelations
yeah

that blues suite
yeah
that peaceful dance
inside a raging tornado
we call
love

Saturday, June 6, 2020
5:37 a.m.

Tupac and Biggie

i heard his name first
juiced for freedom
like digital underground
railroads and
the sonic blasts
of brendas having babies
was that a movie or
was that life and soundcloud as art
homies can call
but what do black
boys do when we are
trapped in concrete
boxes forever ever
forever ever
fear is a prison
but so is fame too
but what is fame
is the only bus ticket
you got to make it
from the cradle
to the grave
made me think of

revolutions won
and revolutions lost
of assata's great expectations
of black panthers
dead and gone
while panther cubs
leak tears made of
napalm and the muscular
tails of charcoal-grey 'hood rats
made me think of
apartheid
winnie and nelson mandela
of run jesse run
of nations of islam
and new africas
blowin' in the wind
say his name
tupac amaru shakur
shining serpent
who is thankful
to be alive in spite of
absent father
imprisoned stepfather
crack cocaine
police raids
and political movements
from one ghetto
to the next

hip-hop
started out in the park
created by black and
brown boys looking
for frederick douglass
the north star
and the perfect
beat
they called him
mc new york in baltimore
a motherless and fatherless
child in the bay area
tupac
who contorted and coiled his voice into
an ebonics symphony
of urban american patois
breakdancing to the malnourished imaginations
of king's and kennedy's poor people's campaigns
tupac
america's most wanted
political rabble-rouser with a drum beat
beats like the invisible hands of motherlands
come
and motherlands gone
but hip-hop also is the
west indies
and latinx folks too
hip-hop is

christopher wallace
son of jamaican immigrants
jamaica where they toasted
and blew out massive sound systems
jamaica where marcus garvey first
painted it black
the fleshless self-esteem
of ex-slaves asking jah
for a boat ride that drops-kicks them in
an un-colonized and an un-gentrified heaven
jamaica that gave us a founding father
of hip-hop kool herc
and half of brooklyn
where brooklyn at
it is right here biggie smalls
cool-posing on an onion-scented street corner
in a tight yoruba prayer circle
they call a cypher
as shorttallfatskinnydamaged bodies
rhyme and shine the shoes of the blues
of palecoconutyellowredbrownjetblack boys
who considered suicide when
rainbows became coalitions
of the haves and the have nots
biggie
the greatest storyteller
never to win a pulitzer
biggie

who contorted and coiled his voice into
an ebonics symphony
of brooklyn patois
breakdancing to the malnourished imaginations
of king's and kennedy's poor people's campaigns
where brooklyn at
it is right here the notorious b.i.g.
because even gangsters trademark
their names into the history books
of godfathers and macks and superflys
where brooklyn at
right there
where grandmaster flowers
and big daddy kane and stetsasonic
and sawed-off shotguns
and crack vials and crippled
public schools wheel-chaired the way
for you
biggie
so that you could
battle royale rhymes
like mario puzo
dry-humping bloody mobsters
and scandalous politicians
and greasy-haired preachers
like don corleone
cupping your chin
the way the devil would cup

death itself
the way bootsy collins would cup and drink
the wet, sultry licks of his guitar
just means you tupac you biggie
trade war stories
the way trump trades war stories
with fascist mirrors at the white house
means you all
got soul
like iceberg slim had sold his soul
where brooklyn at
right next to harlem and east harlem
tupac the places you were born and lived
like baltimore and marin city
and the sunny pot-holed gutters of los angeles
and atlanta
where they birth and bury kings
and call it racial progress
where brooklyn at
in that one time you and biggie
swapped eye sockets and took photos
as friends
together
apart
two black boys about to be their
generation's elvis and buddy holly
their generation's john lennon
and marvin gaye

big yeah like biggie big
peace in the beginning
but then who shot ya
became the soundtrack
for the dirty half dozens
in green camouflaged armor
crooked finger-pointing
contests that turned into
your coast versus my coast
even though ain't nobody own
either coast
but we know they like to
be slave masters and overseers
and loose black boys on each other
like stink-breathed barking dogs
leaping at and gut-bombing marchers
in john coltrane's alabama
except we marching to jail and cemeteries
not toward the moon or the stars or the sun
it is black boys against each other
as poison is poured over
our dream-y american gumbo
hit 'em up
dis you dis your wife dis your life
dis your career
volcano anger stove-boiled by years
of trauma and dear
mamas addicted

to white lines and hypnotic needles
frozen in the medieval times of warriors
as political prisoners
like mutulu like mutulu like mutulu
hypnotized
we eat and swallow ourselves
and each other
the way we eat and swallow watermelon seeds
grow
ride
die
for death
atop death row SUVs
we join elvis in vegas and los angeles
hang lynch mob ropes around our necks like
they are electric kool-aid acid tests
until we are gunned down
in cars
the way elvis sat on that toilet bowl
waiting for his soul
to flush him into
graceland forever ever
born again six months apart
two dead black boys joined at the lips
of hip-hop's smithsonian institution
gone
because they value you more
dead

than alive
gemini twins that you both are
black boys ain't 'spose to live long
we 'spose to live hard fast short painful
the way they rolled up the torture of jesus
and smoked him on the crucifix
until his humiliation
dripped dripped dripped
an old negro spiritual
into the resurrected earth
of the unbelievable
and our eyes slap box with the white jesus
as we wait for this or that black jesus
named makaveli or big poppa
eyesfacesskins don't lie
they are permanent graffiti murals
for the brothers who ain't here
these photos of them
permanent graffiti murals
black white
in living color
teardrops
lonely teardrops
jesus-walking
like raindrops
shaped like bullet shells
sculpted by the sawdust hands of the lawd
the fears I we still carry

around all these years later
like prison chains about our tattooed wrists
wondering where all those
bullets came from
wondering why
we they would kill
black boys who only
want to be
free

Friday, June 1, 2018
10:56 a.m.

Haiku for Black Boys

Richard Wright taught us
Souls will swell like weighted wings
And break down white walls

Saturday, September 18, 2021
5:11 p.m.

Enough

They shoot us
in the back
They shoot us
'cuz we Black
They shoot us
in the bed
They even
shoot us
when we
dead—

Tuesday, August 25, 2020
8:04 a.m.

Baseball

Baseball is the father I wish I had
Me, a boy of Summer and Spring
Like the almighty Casey with his bat
Swinging and missing a cloth-less fastball for strike three
The way he only saw me three times in my life
Him abandoning me and my mother when I was eight
That father hole as mammoth as the heroical soul of Hank Aaron
Fatherlessness filled by those days
I religiously bounced a pink sponge ball off a building wall
Playing catch with myself
Or taking hard swipes like Casey
At balls thrown by no one at all
My ma never played games
Left that to her only child
As she scrunched and conformed
Her body into intentional walks
And brutal hits by wild pitches
hurled at poor brown women
So that she and I would not die before we scored one lonely run
And other than my single mother and welfare and food stamps
Baseball drafted and dragged me into manhood

By the spiked cleats of my Ty Cobb rage
It grew me past white milk dabbed across my top lip
Past the nasty disses of my pleather second baseman's glove
Past my closest cousin's hook slide around our blood and flesh
Past Hemingway's old man and sea tailing a fish and Joltin' Joe
Baseball schooled me on how to bubble-gum my selfie
In the prickly splinters of busted fences
Like August Wilson's Troy Maxson
His life a soiled, raggedy globe with the stitches come a-loose
Hanging from a rope hanging from a tree
Hanging him hanging me
If I forget my birthright of stolen bases and stolen geographies
If I don't understand
Better to have no daddy
Than to have a punch-drunk one pinch-hit for an absent one
If I don't understand that Willie Mays
Sprinted like he was speed-racing the Underground Railroad
Because he was
The wind ripping that cap from his head
His back to the world like Miles Davis'
As he caught freedom in his outstretched mitt
Whirled 'round like a
Shot putter in the Olympics
And flung freedom to his momma and them
In a cotton field of dreams
I want to be Willie Mays
The say hey kid with the coolest swag

I want to be Ken Griffey, Jr.
The boom-bap kid with the coolest swag
Because baseball teaches you
To dive fingertips first into tomorrow
like Ichiro and Fernando Tatís, Jr.
Teaches you to chant praise songs for history and math
Teaches you to collect and tuck yourself into shoeboxes
Teaches you what not to do with a bat
Like that day Columbus clubbed Kojo
Over the head with a Louisville slugger
The lump in the centerfield of Kojo's brain
as towering as the Empire State
Because Columbus' hands were not splendid enough
To make his point plain
Kojo was never the same
After that day he plopped to the earth like a badly missed fly ball
And my folding bed and I brawled for weeks in blank horror
At how my beloved baseball
Could be double played instantly
Like Tinkers to Evers to Chance
By hate and trauma
As in the afternoon I went outside
in my new White neighborhood
to freestyle stickball with the boys
on the block and one of the White
Dudes, a sour-mouthed redhead, insisted on referring to me
as "the n_____" until I chased
him with our stickball bat

from sewer to fire hydrant to the door
of his crib as he crouched like a catcher behind
his mother who swore he meant
no harm whatsoever
Nope, he never called me that word again
But in that moment, I was Jackie Robinson
Bug-spraying my eyes against slavery and segregation
As I baited and bounced like Sammy Davis, Jr. on third base
Then I projected myself, as a nuclear missile, toward home plate
Surgically ahead of Yogi Berra's tag
Jackie was not merely stealing a base
But he was also retracing and reclaiming
The tie-dye teardrops of an Orisha
The ancestral blue door of no return
The antique store memories in Blackface
One basepath at a time
Not knowing that breathing as a Negro in a league of his own would
age and hock-spit him down as it would me years later
God bless you, please, Mrs. Jackie Robinson
Heaven keeps a space for those who slay
Yea, yea, yea—
Yea, yea, yea—
Is that why they evermore photoshop Curt Flood
from the same Mount Rushmore that showcases
racists and drug addicts and
alcoholics and adulterers and cheaters?
Is that Branch Rickey and Curt Flood and Roberto Clemente
I see high five—ing their lives away to spare humankind?

Did Curt Flood's whistle during just a friendly game of baseball
render him the Emmett Till of American sports?
Is this why I can scarcely find boys like me
playing baseball anymore?
Yes, baseball has both healed and bruised me
It has gnarled fingers
dislocated shoulders
permanently scarred knees
I have methodically devoured victory
as if it is my ma's sweet potato pie
I have methodically vomited defeat
as if it is artificial turf in my vegan-buttered popcorn
Baseball is love, is the first great love of my life
My beautiful and bewildering New York Yankees
The concrete paradise in The South Bronx
The uptown funk that the Jazz Age built
When Irish Jewish Italian African American
Puerto Rican West Indian Dominican
Unbraided boy stories the way we traded baseball cards as youth
Digitizing the decades while beat-boxing
the blues, bebop, boogaloo, and Black and Boricua soul:
I am Babe Ruth
A sultan swatting the moon and Mars like they are country-flies
I am Lou Gehrig
An iron horse hobbling hearts with a naked self-eulogy
I am Joe DiMaggio
A quietly regal clipper carving number 56 into baseball's ozone
I am Mickey Mantle

An Oklahoma comet consecrating dust with the swiftest of feet
I am Reggie Jackson
An October Picasso brush-stroking eternity with a simple bat toss
I am Rickey Henderson
A prophet with legs of steel scaling horizons like Baryshnikov
I am Derek Jeter
A private super-man confounding doom with the flip of a wrist
I am Aaron Judge
A hip-hop Paul Bunyan hailing launch angles like the gods themselves
Their seventh inning stretch
Be my Geechee grandma's roots conjuring
Me up from boyhood poverty to attend
My earliest Yankee games
As a grown-up shoulder-to-shoulder with the
eight-year-old me in utter wonderment
Their seventh inning stretch
Be my Geechee grandma's roots conjuring
Me up from the Jim Crow dugout
Of Josh Gibson and "Cool Papa" Bell and **Satchel** Paige
As they serenade America with
"Take Me Out to the Ball Game"
a sing-along as joyful as a Mudville sweaty palm
Gently patting my cheek when I
Proclaimed to the maddened thousands
I would be a big leaguer one day
No, I cannot dream of a world without our national pastime
Yes, baseball is the perfectly imperfect
father I wish I had

And I will
forever be that kid in love with
the sport that saved my life

Wednesday, November 17, 2021
6:00 a.m.

My Father

I forgive you
For leaving me
As a little boy
With a hole the size
Of a jumbo airplane
With no arms
Because you
Did not
Know
How to love
Yourself
I forgive you
For telling my mother
She lied
That you would
Never give her
A near nickel
For me again
Though I did not know
What a near nickel was
I forgive you
For the times

My mother yelled at me
Not to be like you
But then also screamed
I was just like you
I forgive you
For those moments
When my mother
Grabbed and shook me
When she really
Wanted to
Grab and shake you
I forgive you
For all
The graveyard moments
Where I
Wished I was being
Taught by you
How to be a man
But had to
Scan
The different angles
Of blinking eyes of
Some other male life
While they were not looking
I forgive you
For never calling me
After that day you
Bumped into my mother

Years later
And took my telephone number
And said that you would
But never did
I forgive you
For the hurt
Forever lurking there
Like a pipe bomb
In my living room
For the hurt
Forever sleeping there
Like an unwanted partner
In my bedroom
I forgive you
Because I heard how
Years later
On your death march
With a body part or two
Chopped off
Missing
You asked your other children
For me
The only one not there
The only one up North
The only one who had barely ever seen you
The only one who did not know you
The only one who never called you
Dad or pop or sir

I forgive you for dying
Without my knowing
Yet I cried a decade later
When I found out
Because the hole was still there
I forgive you
Because
I also forgive me
For all those many years
I hated myself
For having
No father

Monday, February 7, 2022
8:32 a.m.

Janet Jackson Never Lies

won't wait till she gone
to see what we got
cocoa-creamed queen in a big yellow taxi
mother father nine children
two-bedroom shoebox house
gary, indiana kool-aid acid test
generational trauma passed around
like a stillborn
baby
tucked inside a moth-ridden blanket
god's gracious gift
her nametag
walking miracle
her laundry bag
little girls have dreams too
little girls want control too
super-woman super-star
african songs african griots
kidnappings middle passages
plantations beatings rapes of grown-ish bodies
reconstruction jim crow minstrel shows
black women blamed banished

like they still the un-godly mules of the earth
she smiles anyway she smiles anyway
sugar bowl of color envy malfunctioning
like a tree branch chopping a rope in half
you can shade her resume
but you can't shade her hustle and flow

Sunday, May 16, 2021
9:00 p.m.

When I Found Malcolm X

I shed tears the way a dam
bursts wide open when exposed
by an awful hurricane
that moment at age 18
after the first time I
hungrily ate the words of
The Autobiography of Malcolm X
because I did not
know a Black man
like him could even exist
I cried—hard—because they had
bowed and arrowed
bullet after bullet
into Malcolm the way
hunters murder
a defenseless lion or deer:
he was both a lion and a deer
a lion undaunted by
America's naked jungles
a deer forever thirsty
about what is

underneath the there
they bamboozled
us into believing was freedom
I howled like an unwanted ghetto baby
dumped into the trash bag of history
because in his book
I was able to hold
and hug my own face
for the very first time:
a Black boy ruthlessly damaged
by abuse hate self-hate
mental illness racism
and that violence
we call poverty
I wailed as we had
wailed at those
bluer than blue
church revivals
as the preacher-man
like Malcolm's daddy the preacher-man
made us believe
there was a heaven
for the holes of Black folks—
I went to school like Malcolm
was the Negro mascot like Malcolm
made un-safe love to the streets like Malcolm
was the prison waiting for myself

like Malcolm
I was there when he
was re-born, once more and once more—
I set that book
down and rolled and smoked
his speeches
the way I have been
smoking this joint called life
since my father told my mother
"he ain't my son"
when I was eight years old
I puked fresh buckets
of Ivory soap and muddy waters
because in this dead
Black man
I had found
God—the holy ghost—and the father
I knew
would never forsake me
M-M-M-Malcolm
gave me what
I was missing
he instructed
me to posterize myself
to be nothing but a man
with a stainless-steel backbone
and legs locked into place

like Jesus'
on that march
to that cross

Monday, February 1, 2021
11:07 a.m.

America

Listen at me good, hear?
I ain't but too educated
'bout fourth fifth grade
far as I wents
don't even know
what year I was born
exacts-ly
i can reads good enough
i can counts my money
good enough
And I knows when
somethin' ain't right
ya hear?
I grew up on this land
my daddy share-cropped
I watched him
drop his eyes
to the ground
like he was smashin'
two watermelons
every times
one of them

come his way
He was 'shame
to be hisself
in front of them
I ain't fixin'
to do that
but I don't
wants no trouble either
I heard them
tales 'bout Till
'bout colored
people swingin'
from trees
so I knews
right away not
to do nothin'
that would get me
in trouble
Alls my life
I works hard
I picks cotton
I cuts weeds
I paints houses
I cooks for them
I landscapes for them
I delivers boxes
big as that
sun lookin' like

it 'bout to be eaten
by the devil's clouds
I fought over
there in Vietnam
and came back
with a
bullet in my right leg
That bullet still there
Hurt reals bad
when it rain
yessuh it do
but I ain't never complain
i still worked alls my life
I married my wife
we had five children
four gals and one boy
we made a way
outta no way
all our kids
done somethin'
with they-selves
the grands too
I done retired now
'cuz
I cain't drive no more
I cain't carry boxes no more
arthritis done froze
most my fingers

pretty good
like them chicken parts
we saves and puts
in the freezer
I just sets on this here porch
chewin' my 'bacco
sippin' sweet tea
and I reads my newspaper
sometimes
I gets upset
when I hears
'bout Trump
when I hears
'bout what they
fixin' to do to our votes
'bout what they
did to that boy
up there in Minnesota
how they set they knee
on his neck
he callin' for his
momma
made me have flashbacks
to us callin' for our
mommas
in Vietnam
whenever one of us was 'bout to die
ain't right

how they done us
no
we ain't never bothers
them like that
taint right
that why I just
holds my bible
in my left hand
when I sits on this here porch
every day
gotta stay right
with the Lawd
I prays daily too
like pastor say I should
like my wife say I should
I'm a deacon in my church
ain't miss no Sundays
alls my life
'cept for when
I was in Vietnam
and when the Covid hit
don't know how
much time
I gots left
just happy I had my time
done seen a lot
I don't bothers nobody
I don't hates nobody

just want to
be right
for the Lawd
when it my turn
for the judgment day
I done alls I could
to be ready

Wednesday, November 17, 2021
6:05 a.m.

i am magic

(for Bridget L. Moore)

i am magic
i can do anything
i can moon-walk
my bare feet on fire
and taste sunrise
when others
cannot taste at all
i was born the year
dianne mcintyre
un-buried freedom
from below
an ohio underground railroad
and made new york
her power-to-the-people
dance partner
i was given breath amidst
super fly afros
tent-wide bell bottoms
and soul-trained symphonies
with tightened fists jabbing

and counterpunching
red-white-blues-song tomorrows
i was cornrolled
where cowboys
are dusty-eyed gladiators
slow smoking the ghosts
of devil he-men
who took jfk away
don't matter my momma
had me at 18
don't matter
my momma and me
had to rock and climb
our ancestors' bloodied backs
to find ourselves
what matters
is that black girls
chocolate-brown and true like me
make music with our
movements
before we even kiss
the universe hello
because
for months of sundays
i am my momma's
only child
i sit in a chair
next to my imagination

and i ego trip
and draw
for-coloreds-lonely poetry
like nikki giovanni
for months of sundays
i am my momma's
only child
i sit in a chair
next to my imagination
and i protest
and wait to exhale
slavery and four women like
nina simone
for months of sundays
i am my momma's
only child
i sit in a chair
next to my imagination
and cause blind rebels
to explode inside their heads
like eartha kitt
i am magic
i can do anything
i can moon-walk
my bare feet on fire
and taste sunrise
when others
cannot taste at all

i have no name
like woman or girl
dancer-warrior
stolen from herself
through african doors
of no return
i choreograph
art at the bottom
of them boats
i braid escape
routes in my hair
while swallowing
a trumpet full of cotton
in them fields
i can sing
and i can dance
lawd knows i can sing
and i can dance
like
big momma
like marilyn cox
like "tootha"
like wilma dews
like linda hines
like the way
pearl primus and
katherine dunham
sang with their bodies

reversing slave ships
with their fingers
burning plantations
with their elbows
un-knotting nooses
with their necks
lifting traumatized eyes
with their legs
and reviving
sandra bland
and breonna taylor
with their hips
because
black women
black girls
so dope
we can
sing and dance
and sew and paint
and act and mime
and cook and write
rhythms for a nation
of billions
like janet jackson
or the lady school janitor
who taught me to
dance
at age six

because momma
ain't had no money
for me to take dance
classes
i understood right then and
there
that
art
dance
learning
black girl magic
be like
cicely tyson
sarah vaughan
ella fitzgerald
lorraine hansberry
angela davis
be making a way out of no way
be black women and black girls
strutting through the sky
even when our wings
are barely taped together
because
ain't no love
no families
no communities
no possibilities
no church

no holy ghost
no get-out-the votes
if we ain't here
because
we are magic
we can do anything
we can moon-walk
our bare feet on fire
and taste sunrise
when others
cannot taste at all

Thursday, May 13, 2021
7:11 a.m.

Haiku for Vangie

books are love to us
words pour like milk from our lips
watch this poem drink you

Sunday, January 31, 2021
5:38 p.m.

Valentine Haiku

for Vangie

eye kiss god for you
because you're baptizing me
in your skin's deep sea

Sunday, February 14, 2021
7:14 a.m.

For You

I could stare at you all day
Even in pitch blackness
You are a beautiful genius—
I draw you with the soft fingers
Around my heart
We make funny faces
With our bare feet
Laughter is the lotion
We put on our bones
After the shower
Our eyes make love
Like two birds
Twirling in a field of passion
I have never met anyone
Like you in my life
I am both excited and terrified
Excited because we have been here before
Perhaps in post-war Paris
Or the Harlem Renaissance
Two lovers swaying to jazz
And French-kissing history
While reading Zora and Langston to each other

Terrified because we are the children
Of families long abused and traumatized
We don't want to be married to destruction
We want to be free
To write love poems with our bath water
We want to be free
To burn and sage the past with our tears
This is what we dream
As our words hug tight each other
Inside the belly
Of our imagination

Saturday, June 5, 2021
7:44 a.m.

Love

I adore you
I like you
You are my best friend
May I make love
To your eyes?
May I taste
The heaven-dipped
Mango at the
Edges of your mouth?
Can I be a green
Hummingbird
Sleeping in your soul?
May I, please?
Can I, please?
Forgive me
If I tell you
I love you
Too much
Forgive me
If I want
To stand
In love with you

Bury my heart
In the angel's halo
That is your face
Hold hands with
You for the next
Fifteen thousand years
And dance with you
Until our feet
Tattoo our names
Into that part
Of the moon
We call us

Sunday, October 17, 2021
6:31 p.m.

Jamaican Love Poem

I will never stop telling you
that I love you

Like this powdery-blue sky
will never not ooze
its pigment into the Caribbean Sea

We are one like the sky and the sea

Hug and hold me, my love
The way a nine-mile Rastafarian
holds and hugs humanity
with their poetic patois

Save and change my life, my love
Yes, you have, yes, you have—

The way the Maroons
changed and saved their own lives
By bolting to the high mountains
Atop the shoulders of Jamaican blackbirds
and unnamed Taino relatives

Dream of me as I dream of you, my love
Like we did at that plantation house
they call Rose Hall

Not even the legend of Annie Palmer
can stop me and you
from sneaking kisses as we machete sugar cane
with tongues thickened by akee and rice and peas

My belly is full, my love/I have never been this content
Please, let me place my head on your chest
I want to rest
until Marcus Garvey's boat
returns us to the land of mothers and okra and pepper pot soup—

Yet I must rush through the black and sleepy night—

Then I can wake to a floating brown gazebo in your eyes
Then I can wake to our feet intertwined like the roots of a Blue Mahoe tree

And then I can match God's joy each time I awaken to your smile

Wednesday, December 22, 2021
6:43 p.m.

A Love Sonnet

I've waited a life for a love like yours
It appeared as a red moon from the south
I feel warm fingers orbiting my pores
I taste joy at the corners of your mouth

I did not know that I was mad hungry
That I was this starved for a simple touch
My love, I must enjoy this reverie
From bone to skin I adore you so much

Our legs interlaced like rope when we rest
Hearts race each other like African drums
I've laid burdens upon the sun's bare chest
I've blown the tops off mountains with your lungs

Together we jump the broom's tulip floor
And when we die, I'll love you even more

Wednesday, December 29, 2021
9:12 a.m.

Bonus Tracks

for aunt cathy

life ain't never been promised to nobody
that's what grandma lottie used to say
and you
her youngest daughter
and youngest of six children
snuck into the city
on a greyhound bus
with my mother
and scraped the side of a boarding house for good luck
as your life stretched beyond
the wooden shacks
and cotton fields
and the sandy school room floors of south carolina

and you were alive
at last
free
in a city
away from the
comforting stench of down south
and in the big city
with its

musty underarm
and gasoline breath

and you took all ten years of your schoolin'
and applied for a job as a factory worker
on the assembly line
and you assembled parts
and the parts assembled you into
the permanence of minimum wages
and time clocks
and bosses who thought a black woman
was supposed to like work
hell, y'all had been conditioned to be oxes
they figured

and when you wasn't producing like an ox
their tucked-in pot bellies would ask:
why you moving so slow cathy?
and on the inside you licked your tongue
at them the way you used to do
when my mother and my aunt birdie yelled at you
and your heart tightened around your waist
and you ate what your feet could produce
for eight hours a day
40 hours a week
with
one 15 minute break a day
if you was doing your job

and you needed something else
to keep your tears from spitting out
thoughts and words that would send you
back down south
in a fit of fear
and you met him
and he was fine
that man
and you liked him
and he liked you
and like became love
to you
and like became lust
for him
and he and you
exploded into anthony
my cousin anthony
one april day in 1966
and now you had a shield
to hold against the world
you had a world to shield you against
the heartaches of him
the foot aches of work
and the headaches
of city life

and you raised anthony
the best way you knew how

just like my mother raised me
and anthony grew and i grew
with our frustrated imaginations
to resent each other
to hate you, our mothers
to despise our very existences
in that tiny
cramped three-room apartment
two mothers and two sons
in a three-room apartment
held together
by welfare
food stamps
and the roaches
who always found their way
into our food
no matter how thick
the layers of aluminum foil

and that thirsty, tingling sensation
would often reappear
crawling between your toes
up your legs
across your thighs
teasing your crotch
but it couldn't get any further
that's nasty,

you thought,
some man between my legs
again
so you stuffed your womb
with the world of anthony
because your spirit
was tired of being probed
by social workers, mailmen, and would-be husbands
for having an illegitimate son

and in spite of reality
burning down every hope we had
we managed to spread out
to a better part of the ghetto
and we even had separate apartments now
but you and my mother
always was in the same building because
my mother was the mean one
who scoffed at the world
with her angry eyes
and you was the nice one
who wanted to be like my mother
but you couldn't
so you followed my mother
everywhere
because at least you'd be safe
from yourself

and when we finally moved out of the ghetto
around white folks
you felt good
we was movin' up
and flying like birds released from their mother's grip for the
first time
and we was happy to be around
white folks
and didn't mind being called niggas
because at least we was good niggas

and me and anthony
knocked off the weight of
that restless city
that dirty city
and we left:
me to college
anthony to the navy
leaving you and my mother
grazing in the pastures of mid-life

and my mother was happy to be free of a man-child
but you was sad
because anthony had been your reason to live
your reason to work
your reason to exist
and now his departure meant your death
and you were dying

a slow death
dancing with mid-life and dying a muted death
the years of working were gone
the years of sharing were gone
the years of being were gone
and the woman inside of your crouching body
died one may day in 1988 when grandma lottie was buried
and as we wiped the tears from our eyes
no one noticed you sinking through the church pew
through the floor
into the earth to join grandma lottie

and even though anthony was there at the funeral
he left again
back to the navy
back to japan
to some strange place
that was not him
because he hated himself
and he hated you
for being him
and he nailed shut
the door
on your life

and no one noticed you drowning in your pain
until you began having conversations with yourself
and tellin' everyone how you was hearing things

and seeing movies on your living room wall
how you was the star in those movies

and even my mother
with her superstitious ways
could not believe
that you were a victim of roots and magic spells

and my mother and aunt birdie did it;
they tricked you with a meal and had you straight-jacketed
and they didn't tell me
but i found out and i found you
and i leaped inside your body
and begged you to wake up
i swam inside your dried up tears
and turned back the currents
to your childhood
to your adolescence
to your early adulthood
to anthony
to anthony's father
to my mother and aunt birdie and grandma lottie
and i cried between the lines of your history

and you told me you were not crazy
and i said i know
and you told me you could not understand

why my mother and aunt birdie had put you there
and i said i know
and you told me how they drugged you
how they called you by a number
how they monitored your phone calls
and i knew that you had become a prisoner of your worst fears
            of your own death

and i looked at you and i didn't see you
instead i saw an old black woman
inside your 45-year-old body
and i wanted to rush to you and shake your youth
out of that impostor

but it was you . . .

and now i understand those sounds you heard
and those movies you saw on your walls
you are not crazy
it took me a long time
but i understand
anthony knows what you've been through
but he doesn't know you
i know you
my mother and aunt birdie know what you've been through
but they don't know you
i know you

i carry you with me every day
i see you when i see that black woman
lying on the ground with a mcdonald's cup in her hand
at 34th street
i see you and i say
"here cathy,
this is all i got"
and i drop a tear into your cup
and curse myself and my mother and aunt birdie
and anthony and anthony's father
and i kiss you with a prayer
because now i understand
why black bodies sag the way they do
and why black hearts don't birth emotions anymore

1990

Reality Check

For Kurt Cobain
(1967–1994)

i hate myself and want to die

i can hear you saying that now

the words like gunshots blasted into

the skin silencing the nightmares of a

generation we are not an x or twenty-

something

there is more to our teen spirit

it smells like distorted childhoods

and diapered friendships and parents

who fed us watergate and vietnam

and ronald reagan and saturday morning

cartoons without giving us a love we could

grip and suck on when the earth

was burning in our direction

and now you are gone

nah! i refuse to believe that

a whole bunch of us were gonna go and listen to you

regurgitate our blues (yours too) and make anxiety-filled

guitar licks into a futuristic rock opera (our opera)

your hair would fly like a stringy flag saluting the knuckleheads of

the world, yes! us! the post-civil-rights post-vietnam post-reagan

babies would somehow feel validated when your hoarse, garbled

tongue slapped the world with an indictment that said "you have

neglected us for too long and look, just look at what you have created" and we would mosh and slam-dance, our bodies contaminated with

this thing called youth, into a fitful overdose (isn't that what they expect of

us anyhow?) of icon-worshipping you: but you are

alive!

tongue-kissing your feminine side on saturday night live

alive!

eating environmentally-sound fruit next to river phoenix

and you whisper in james dean's ear

as janis, jimi, jim and john, the post-

happy days mount rushmore,

fall stone in love with the grunge thing

and someone will fanzine you

and call you a tragic genius

and bury you in mtv heaven

because no one no one no one

will ever understand why your flannel shirts

and ripped jeans and busted guitars mean

you have loved and lived much longer

than most of us . . .

1994

September 11th

Might it be, as my mother said to me on this ugly, sinful day,
That the world is on its last go-round?
Hijacked wild birds strip the sky of its innocent morning breath
Steel towers crumple like playing cards on an uneven metal table
Unrehearsed screams we dare not hear leap from windows
Into the open, bottomless palms of God
I cannot stand to watch life reduce
Itself to powdery dust and soot lathering the devil's inflamed mouth
But I am fixated on the television anyhow:
Is this what slavery was like?
Is this what the holocaust was like?
Is this what famine is like?
Is this what war is like?
Is this how you felt, dear mother, when King and the two Kennedys were killed?
I want to stitch up the sky, deny humans the right to fly
Cry until my tears have washed hatred
From the mildewed underarms of history
And I want to say to the firemen
Ah, yes, the firemen:
Your husband, your father, your brother, your uncle, your friend
Thank you for speeding to the end of
Your time and thank you for showing us that

Courage is a soul so unselfish it would
Scale a collapsing building to liberate a stranger
Even as your blood relatives wonder if you are alive —
From the remains of this madness
I detect a heartbeat called life
From the remains of this madness
I smell an aroma called love
From the remains of this madness
I embrace a body called humanity
From the remains of this madness
I construct a dream called hope
From the remains of this madness
I will ride the wings of the deceased
Into the clouds, scribble their names on the sun,
Erect a memorial to the moon, chant the blues
For New York City, then resurrect a world
Where a new-born rose will jut through the broken concrete.

November 2001

Son2Mother

Mother, have I told you

That you are the first woman
I ever fell in love with, that what
I've always wanted in life is to hear
You say you love me, too?

That is why, ma, it has taken
Me so long to write this poem.
For how could I, a
Grown man, put words to paper
If I am that little boy
Cowering beneath the power of
That slap, the swing of that belt,
Or the slash and burn of that switch
You used to beat me into fear and submission?

I constantly cringe, ma,
When I think of that oft-repeated chorus you sung
As a fusillade of blows walloped my skeleton body:
Are you gonna be good? Are you gonna be good?

Sometimes when I call you these days, mother,
I just don't know what to say, thus I fall silent,
Even when you ask "How are you doing?"
I want to give you real talk,
Tell you that I am still that stunted only child
Traumatized by the violence of your voice;
That I am still that shorty too terrified to fall
Asleep for fear of your pouncing on me
The moment I shut my eyes—
And you did, mother, again and again,
Until I could no longer sleep peacefully
As a child, and I have never actually had
Many tranquil nights of sleep since.
I lay awake sometimes, as an adult,
Thinking someone is going to get me,
Going to strike me, going to kill me
Because of those heart-racing hours
Of darkness far far ago.

And I remember that time I ran under
Our bed, and in your titanic rage
You tore the entire bed apart,
The frame falling on one of my legs,
And there I was, stuck, mother,
And you ripped into me anyhow.
And oh how I howled for mercy.
But there was none, mother.
Yet there was that chorus:

Are you gonna be good? Are you gonna be good?
And I really did not know, mother, what being good meant.
Nor what you wanted me to be.
Because one day I thought you loved me
And the next day I thought you hated me.

And I did not know back in the day, ma,
That you had been assaulted and abused
The same way, by my granddaddy,
Your father, a 19th century son of ex-slaves
who would break you and your
Three sisters and brother down with mule whips,
With soda bottles, with his gnarled hands—
That he was an embittered mister,
That you were the child who became
Most like your father. Do you not
Recall that past, mother?
I am saying you once chided me,
After you learned I had struck someone as an adult,
To keep my hands to myself, and I wanted to say
But, ma, why didn't you keep your hands to yourself?
Why didn't you command your hands, your arms,
To hug me, instead of urging them to damage me?

And that is what I previously was, ma: damaged
Goods that liked living on the other side of midnight.
That is why, mother, there was no sleep for me till Brooklyn,
Because I needed to escape the concrete box

Needed to escape the mental terrorism
Needed to escape you and that
Paranoid schizophrenic existence.
I am not crazy, ma. I know
Our destinies were frozen in those days
When we shared
That bed and room together,
Because we were too poor
To afford a full apartment.
To those days, mother, when I
Thought you were the bravest
Human being on earth as you
Fought super-sized black rats with
Your broomstick, or effortlessly
Shooed the army of roaches away
From our dinner table—

Maybe, ma, I have not been
Able to write this poem
Because I can envision you as a
Young mother, the one who suitcased
Her dreams when you left South
Carolina, when you moved, first, to Miami
To create a new life for yourself, to flee
The world that murdered your
Grandfather, a local cook, by stuffing food in his mouth,
Then baptizing him in cracker water and proclaiming
It was an accident. It was the world that knocked

On your grandmother's door and told
Her she had to give up 397 of those 400 acres
Of land called the Powell Property—
One penny for each acre of land—
And what your grandmother was left with
Was a jar of soil called Shoe Hill,
The contaminated hill where you were born, ma:
That world never bothered to change the
Name from the Powell Property. And there you
Were, at age eight, sunrising with the moldy men
And the wash-and-wear women
As God's yawn and morning stretch
Tickled the rooster's neck,
Waking you good colored folks to toil on that Powell Property—
To pick cotton for White folks as if being
Cheap and exploited labor was your American birthright.

And you were angry bye and bye, mother.
You would get so angry, Aunt Birdie told me
One time, that sweat droplets would form on your nose,
Your brow would curl up, and the world and
Anyone in it would become your
Empty lard can to kick back and forth up the road a piece.
Ah, ma, but you were such a pretty little Black
Girl—I have the picture right here this minute,
Of you at 12 or 13, tender and dark ebony skin
A beautiful yet temperamental and unloved Black girl
Told that you were ugly, that you had ugly hair,

That you would never be anything other than
The help and wooden steps for someone else's climb—

But you were persistent, ma, and mad determined
To make something of yourself.
And Jersey City
Welcomed you as it welcomed each of
The lost-found children of the Old South
Welcomed y'all country cousins to
Number runners slumlords
Pimps drug dealers bad credit
Huge debts and would-be
Prophets who called themselves storefront preachers
And there you were, mother, within a year,
With my father—

Was he your first love, ma, did he mop
The Carolina clay from your feet?
Did he sprinkle sweet tea and lemon on your belly?
Did he ever really make love to you, mother?
Or was he more like that plantation robot
Who was built to mate then make a quick
Dash to the next slave quarters?
What I do know, mother, is that you went to the hospital
Alone, to spread your legs for
A doctor whose plasma face you do not remember
To push forth a seed you had attempted
To destroy twice because you feared his

Birth would mean the death of you.
But there I was, ma, in your arms
Screaming lunging fleeing
And you were so tremendously ashamed
To be an unwed mother that you did
Not tell Grandma Lottie for five years,
Until that day we showed up
In your hometown of Ridgeland, South Carolina.

But what a mother you were:
You taught me to talk
Taught me to know my name
Taught me to count to read to think
To aspire to be something.
You, my grade-school educated mother,
Gave me my swagger—
Told me I was going to be a lawyer or a doctor,
Told me I was going to do big things,
That I was going to have a better life
Than this welfare this food stamp this government cheese
Had pre-ordained for us.
And we prayed, mother, yes lawd we prayed—
To that God in the sky, to the White Jesus on our wall,
To the minister with the good hair and the tailored suits,
To the minister with the gift
To chalk on busted souls and spit game in foreign tongues—
And back then, ma, I did not understand the talking in tongues
The need to pin pieces of prayer cloth on our attire

The going to church twice a week
The desperation to phone prayer hotlines when there was trouble.
But what you were doing, ma,
Was stapling our paper lives together as best you could
Making a way out of no way
Especially after my father announced,
When I was eight,
That he would not give "a near nickel" to us again.
And he never did, mother, never—

And I sometimes wonder if that is when
The attacks got worse because you were
So viciously wounded
By my father's ignorance and brutality
That that ignorance and brutality
Was transferred to me
As you would say, in one breath,
Don't be like your father
And in another
You just like your no-good daddy

And, yes, I am crying this second, mother,
As I write this poem
Because I see you today:
A retired Black woman with a limp, a bad leg,
Shuffling up and down three flights of stairs.
Too headstrong to allow me to move
You from that heat-less apartment,

Life reduced to trips to the grocery store
A bus ride to the mall
A sacred pilgrimage to the laundry room
And the daily ritual of judge shows, Oprah, and the local news.

And, mother, you remain without the love you forever
Crave, and you forever speak of getting married one day.
And you are so very worn out from
Fifty-four years of back breaking work—
But this I know now:
Your life was sacrificed so that I could have one, ma.

So I write this poem, son to mother, to say I love you
Even if you refuse to accept my words
Because you are too afraid to defeat the devil
And bury the past with our ancestors once and for all.
I write this poem
To say I forgive you for everything, mother—
For the poverty for the violence for the hunger
For the loneliness for the fear
For the days when I blamed you for my absent father
For the days when I wanted to run away
For those days when I really did run away—
I forgive you, ma, for those days you cursed
And belittled me, for those days when you said
I was never gonna make it.
Oh, yes, ma, I do forgive, I forgive you for
The beatings, I do, dear mother, I do—

Because if it were not for all of who you are
All of where you come from
All of what you created for me
I would not be alive today.

For below the bloody scar tissues of your fire and fury
And aggravations and self-imposed house arrest
Is a woman who defied the mythmakers
Turned her nose up at the doomsayers—
Is someone who fought landlords
And crooked police officers and
Social workers and school systems and
Deadbeat men who wanted to live off of
Her; and from the tar and feathered remains
Of lives noosed from the very beginning,
We have survived, and here we are, mother:
You have never said you love me
But I know every time I come home
And you've made potato salad and stringbeans,
Every year you've mailed me a birthday card
Or asked if you should buy me pajamas for Christmas,
I know that you are,
In your own wildly unpredictable way,
The greatest love I've ever had in my life—

Tuesday, January 1, 2008
8:28 a.m.

Acknowledgments

There is simply no way this poetry collection would exist without the vision, kindness, generosity, and community spirit of the following amazing human beings: Mensah Demary, editor; Andy Hunter, publisher; Nicole Caputo, creative director; Megan Fishmann, director of publicity; Wah-Ming Chang, senior managing editor of production; Evangeline Lawson, photographer; Hilary VanWright, graphic designer; Regan Richardson and Michael Cohen, literary eagle eyes; and Billy Johnson, Jr., my personal publicist. Also, I must say thank you very much to everyone with Soft Skull Press/Penguin Random House: You are appreciated. Finally, and first, both, to the spirit(s), the holy spirit(s), the ancestral spirit(s), without whom this book could not have been written by me. I am just a vessel—

Self-Portrait

only child of geechee south carolina super-shero
ya, south carolina holds me down
like sweet potato and watermelon hold me down
born and raised in jersey
with daily poverty as a form of violence
ma had to be momma and daddy
did best she could roamin' from 'hood to 'hood
pitstop at rutgers
booted into reality
became a man in brooklyn
in love with books since a silenced/silent kid
in love with writing bcuz of hemingway/shakespeare/poe
to me writing is breathing
to me writing is therapy
to me writing is the freedom train
to me art is activism and activism is art
done a few books been a few places made a few coins
been married divorced flat broke nearly choked
now prefer sucker-free life
me a seasoned vegan animal-loving brotha
eye love hip-hop
& jazz

& classical
& classic rock
& laughter loads of laughter
eye love skateboarding
& biking
& hiking
& sports loads of sports
I breathe meditate do yoga
I breathe bobby kennedy and malcolm x
I breathe bell hooks and v and frida kahlo and yuri kochiyama
I breathe cuz someone once said I can't

KEVIN POWELL'S PREVIOUS BOOKS

2020: *When We Free the World* (essays); Amazon and Apple Books

2020: *My Mother. Barack Obama. Donald Trump. And the Last Stand of the Angry White Man* (essays); Atria/Simon & Schuster

2015: *The Education of Kevin Powell: A Boy's Journey into Manhood* (autobiography); Atria/Simon & Schuster

2012: *Barack Obama, Ronald Reagan, and the Ghost of Dr. King: Blogs and Essays* (essays); lulu.com

2009: *Open Letters to America* (essays); Soft Skull Press

2008: *The Black Male Handbook: A Blueprint for Life* (as editor, with foreword by Hill Harper); Atria/Simon & Schuster

2008: *No Sleep Till Brooklyn* (poetry); Soft Skull Press

2006: *Someday We'll All Be Free* (essays); Soft Skull Press

2003: *Who's Gonna Take the Weight? Manhood, Race, and Power in America* (essays); Three Rivers Press/Random House

2002: *Who Shot Ya? Three Decades of Hiphop Photography* (as editor, with photographs by Ernie Paniccioli); HarperCollins

2000: *Step into a World: A Global Anthology of the New Black Literature* (as editor); John Wiley & Sons

1997: *Keepin' It Real: Post-MTV Reflections on Race, Sex, and Politics* (essays); Ballantine/Random House

1995: *recognize* (poetry); Harlem River Press

1992: *In the Tradition: An Anthology of Young Black Writers* (as editor, with Ras Baraka); Harlem River Press

© Michael Scott Jones

KEVIN POWELL is a poet, journalist, civil and human rights activist, filmmaker, and author of fourteen books. He is also a former two-time candidate for the United States Congress in Brooklyn, New York, his adopted hometown. His first documentary as director, writer, and producer, *When We Free the World*, is an exploration of healthy manhood versus toxic manhood through the lens and lives of Black males. Additionally, Powell curated the very first exhibits in America on the history of hip-hop at the Rock and Roll Hall of Fame and Brooklyn Museum, and he was the official U.S. ambassador for the centennial celebration of Welsh writer Dylan Thomas. His writings have appeared in *The New York Times*, NPR, *The Washington Post*, CNN, *Essence*, *Rolling Stone*, *Vibe*, ESPN, *Esquire*, and *The Nation*, among other publications. His next book will be a biography of Tupac Shakur.